for
Evan S

Mary Ranks

Jeannette 3/20/11

Paulette Rochelle-Levy

Dancing
with the
Dívine
Prayers & Meditations
for
Movement & Stillness

ॐ

CREATIVE PATH PRESS

Paulette Rochelle-Levy

Dancing with the Divine:

Prayers & Meditations
for
Movement & Stillness

To order:
(310) 453-4053
or Email to:
creativepath@earthlink.net
www.creativepathwithpaulette.com

Front Cover: **River Morning**, 1995   (30" x 40")
Paulette Rochelle-Levy

Book Cover Design: Leslie Cabarga
www.lesliecabarga.com
Back Cover Photograph: Evans Brown
www.evansbrown.com

For my parents,

Rabbi Paul Richman and Miriam B. Richman,
for their continual presence in my life and work

Paintings
by
Paulette Rochelle-Levy

Table of Contents

God, distill me to pure essence
That I may hear your prayers for me.

INTRODUCTION

My Journey

These whispers, callings, strugglings, shoutings and dancings are intimate expressions of the relationship with my beloved God. The paintings, interwoven throughout, are my responses to skies, trees, mountains and water that have blessed me on my way.

I have a deep memory:

My rabbi father, draped in a black robe, is raising his arms blessing the congregation, blessing me, with *Y'varechecha*, the final benediction:

"May God shine His Light upon you.
And bring you peace. "

With this prayer the service was concluded. Like a cord, this memory pulls me back to Daddy, Father God, and my ancestors.

However, so many of the other traditional prayers to the patriarchal "Lord God King of the Universe" left me distanced, bored and restless. Half in Hebrew, a beautiful but foreign language, half in unpoetic English, the prayers lacked sweetness and passion.

I now view those prayers as Judaism without juice! These were praises to God who was busy holding up the moon and the stars and surely did not have time for me. Religious school was boring; the Bible stories had nothing to do with me and the struggles of my young life. Jewish holidays were a series of "shoulds," of ritual that was proper, but had no soul.

In general, religion was oppressive and irrelevant. Where was the oneness I felt when I climbed the willow tree, the purity that I felt when I swam my lake in New Hampshire? Where was the enthusiasm that moved through me when I was dancing? Or the joy that I felt when I was painting?

And, then too, this God seemed so cruel. When I was six, God took my mother just as she was giving birth to what would have been another brother. Unfortunately, my distraught father told me she would return – "God just wanted to talk to her for awhile." I waited and waited for her return. When she didn't re-appear I became seriously depressed. Then, when I was thirteen my father died also. My uncle, whom we had gone to live with after our father's death, passed away four years later. I found myself crying out, "If God is so cruel how can there be a God?"

A few short years later, I was given the gift of carrying new life. At nineteen, I was in love, married and birthing my first beautiful daughter. Three years later we were blessed with another precious daughter.

So, quite early in life, I was given experiences of the boundaries of life –Death and Birth – along with lots of profound questions.

There is a Native American saying, "Tragedy comes with gifts in the other hand." In retrospect, I can perceive that there were gifts in these early losses. I have found my way from fear to faith.

I have learned great and difficult lessons as I moved from a hurting heart to one of such tremendous love. Healing the traumas of the past showed me the possibilities of transformation, which I could pass on to others. Empathy for those in pain laid the groundwork for becoming a therapist. Being on my own at a young age gave me survival skills of independence and tenacity. I realized that for years when faced with a dilemma I would ask myself, "How would Huck Finn do it?" Like Huck Finn, I know I can count on my own ingenuity!

My adult life became more charged with responsibility. A progressively difficult marriage incorporated with the intense tasks of being a full-time student while mothering, found my body aching with continual tension. I sought out the deep-tissue work of Rolfing to cleanse myself of years of suppressed body memory and to soften the tight muscles of my dancer's body, in addition to psychotherapy, to heal emotional pain. I learned to meditate and to practice yoga.

I had sought out meditation as a simple relaxation technique. And, fortunately, I had tools to carry me through the ending of my marriage and the stressors of becoming a single mother.

Little did I know the worlds that meditation practice would open for me. Meditation opened the door to Energy healing. Becoming a channel of Energy was a huge spiritual awakening. To sense the Presence of healing in hands and heart and to transmit that to people in pain - to become that kind of instrument, was a humbling and awesome gift. Inspired by this Mystery, I became a massage/movement therapist.

How graced I have been to continually work with people as a vehicle for dancing with the Divine.

After further education I became a psychotherapist and a teacher. My work is a continual training in the skills of intuition. I am always learning to listen, not just to what people are saying with words and to perceive not only how their bodies speak but also to intuit all that is left unsaid. And, to intuitively hear God within, who is always here to guide me. This is the place that I do a therapy session from, teach from and create dances from.

I don't want to take for granted the privilege of being a woman living in this time and place in history. The strength of my feminine power underlines my journey in sexuality, of being a mother and now, as grandmother. Surely, this power provides the fuel for the most dynamic aspects of my spiritual journey.

Always there has been art in some form. A student gave me a sequined pin with the words, "Art saves lives." Creativity carried me through the hardest times of my childhood in the form of dance, painting, sculpting and especially acting which transported me into safer worlds. Exploration and artistic discovery have enriched my world in myriad ways.

My training and performance work as an improvisational dancer has been with me since I was three years old. Dance gives me flexibility, strength, creativity and healing. And connection.

Painting gives me the delight of exploration of color and form. Through the magic of the brush I am transported into new places and perceptions. The paintings are recollections of my time in places like

Topanga, Taos, Kauai, and Big Sur. These sacred sites have fed me deeply.

I was brought back into Judaism when I found a rabbi who made Judaism relevant and sensual. I discovered spiritual aspects of Judaism that embody mysticism and beauty. This path of Jewish Renewal embodies music, dance and meditation as intimate dialogue with the Divine.

The cord that connected me to my father pulled me back. At last, I could come Home.

My life has become a series of intimacies expressed through family, friendships and creative work. Even in the loneliest moments, some connections have always kept me close to the One. Touching a tree, hiking a mountain, watching the rhythm of waves, and gazing into the eyes of my cat have kept me grounded in the path of beauty.

There have been angels in my life – protectors, healers, children, and teachers – who have embodied the Divine, each dancing in his and her way. These people have lit the path for me.

The writing of this book is a summary of sixty years of being lost and found, of songs, dances and paintings, of running to and from, of loss and of abundance, of loneliness and solitude. It has been a journey of questioning the mysteries and ultimately, of learning to love the questions as much as the answers.

I embrace every part that has made me whole, healed and holy.

This book is celebration, gratitude and lovesong.

Let these words be touchstones on your journey.

May your heart be open.

The Value of Prayer and Meditation

Einstein said, "I want to know God's mind. The rest are details." How the mind of God creates the universe remains the ultimate mystery.

Through prayer, meditation and prayerful dance our edges become softer, more permeable. Our minds become quiet. We are able not just to hear, but also to really listen.

Our bodies realign, becoming harmonious, as our breath eases.

Experiment with faith. Play with prayer. You may find yourself enchanted by the power of something so simple-though not always so easy.

God is as close as your breath,
As near as your heartbeat.

Acknowledgments

I acknowledge all of my teachers. I appreciate each of my students and clients with whom I have shared union with the Divine. They, too, have been my teachers. Many of them have received this work with dynamic receptivity, making use of the prayers and meditations in individual ways.

Especially I thank Rabbi Stan Levy of B'nai Horin, Los Angeles. He has been my friend and mentor, supporting and guiding me in bringing this book to fruition. He has encouraged the use of dance as prayer in the garden of Shabbat and in the temple on High Holy Days.

I have been privileged to have my mind turned upside down by Ram Dass in long spiritual retreats.

Others who have kindly given this work their attention have been Rami Shapiro, Don Singer, Stephen Robbins and Edward Zerin, all rabbis with valuable insights.

Jeanette Shelburne and Davida Wendorf, my dear friends, have read the work as it evolved. Leslie Carbarga advised me in the process of book production. Paul and Carol Pines lent me the solitude of their home in upstate New York so I could write.

Jim Stewart with his swift fingers on the keys has freed me to write poetry in longhand. His keen editing has kept me honest. Nancy Seid provided with sensitive editing and proofreading.

Leslie Cabarga helped make this 2011 edition sparkle with his eye for detail and new cover design.

Dan at Printland treated this book with reverence.

Joel and Bill at America's Press, bent over backwards to satisfy my every desire for perfection in printing.

With The Surprise Dance Theatre, I directed and produced some of the poetry as improvisational dance pieces on March 24, 2002. The dancers and musicians Nomi Kleinmuntz, Lynne Fuqua, Gillian McGinty, Andy Wang, Fred Kahane, Frankie Hernandez, David Sonnenshein and vocalist Shirley Harris breathed new life into the words – bringing kinesthetic and musical dimensionality into the prayers.

My family, including Anne Levy, my daughters Willow Lynne Evans and Michelle McMillan, my aunt Helaine Blum and especially, my grandson Zachary, all give me a constant sense of stimulation, joy and comfort.

It has been satisfying to sit with Stephen Mitchell's Psalms of David and the poetry of Rumi, Hafiz, Rilke, Hildegarde of Bingen and many others who came my way to guide me into ecstatic prayer.

Mostly, I say,
Thank you God,
For the blessings of creativity,
For this Time.
You are all I am.

I. *LOVE SONGS TO GOD*

Lovesongs

At last I can fall in love with God – knowing true ecstasy. Did I always know it could be so easy? Perhaps as a child I knew, but like many of us, I have had to find my way Home again.

Now it seems so simple:

Wake up.
Go outside
Stand on the earth
Breathe the air
And say, "Thank you."

Often, I ask myself, "Where is the love in this moment?" Try asking yourself this question. It will awaken you to the goodness amidst harshness, the teaching in a struggle, the blessing even where there is loss.

Let yourself be child-like in the knowing of beauty. Find ways to celebrate by creating your own love songs to God through voice, dance, and gifts of words and action.

Remember joy and gladness; find that which is holy in every moment.

Let yourself fall in love with the Beloved
who is already passionately in love with you.

Beloved God

Open my heart to this day
Unfold the wings of Spirit
That I may greet this moment
Unabashedly naked in joy.

❧

Beloved God

Let me dissolve into you, my Beloved
So there is only being
No striving nor separation
Only Being with You
Only You
Only One

❧

Beloved God

Standing on this earth

Lifting my arms and touching sky

Earth, air, trees, water become me.

Your blessing becomes me

I am Your blessing

This moment is God's blessing

I walk in gladness.

(Ah — Ah — Ah.)

(Ah — Ah — Ah — men.)

༄

Miracles

"There are only two ways to live your life; one is as though nothing is a miracle, the other is as if every-thing is."

Albert Einstein

We are sent miracles all the time. We tend to call a miracle that which is unexpected and seems beyond the realm of possibility. But how do we know all that is possible?

Some of the most extraordinary miracles are quite ordinary and natural. Miracles may be gifts such as the growth of a giant redwood from a tiny seed, the ancient wisdom that comes from a sick child who heals us with his poetry. It may be as magnificent as the planet's continual turning each dawn toward the sun. Or a miracle may be as simple as just the right person showing up at just the right time.

God is praying for us all the time in so many forms, blessing us and sending us gifts. Whatever form God's prayers take, we are charged with the task of being open and available to God.

God is always here.
Where are you?

Miracles in Every Moment

Open my heart

Open my mind

Open my eyes

Open my hands

I receive the miracles

You create in every moment.

❧

II. *THE CALLING*

Walking the Path

We are all called upon to be who we truly are. We have time for nothing less.

Each soul wants to be known to its person. Each person has the birthright of expression and creativity. And with this gift of expression comes the responsibility to the gift. Everyone has specific tasks in each phase of life: to grow, create, serve, build, and love in our own unique way. We are all artists in the creation of our own lives.

Yet, sometimes we are lost on the path. We may be confused about what we are called on to do or be or where to go or how to get to our destination.

Listen very deeply. Ask God to give you the vision to see your path, to know your direction. And, once you know what your calling is, ask that you may have the courage to take the steps to do the work that is required.

The prayer on the next page creates the energy of strong intention.

Vision with strength creates intention.

Intention is the first step on the path to courage.

God, Give Me the Vision

Oh God, give me the vision
To see my path,
And the courage
To walk upon it.

❧

Listen, Listen, Listen

One day when my grandson and I were walking in the woods, he asked me, "Uma, who do you think paints better? You or God?"

Once I had caught my breath from this overwhelming question, I responded, "At one time I felt that God had made nature so perfectly that it was arrogant of me to try to put it on a canvas.

"Then I came to realize that by making paintings of mountains, water and rocks, I was actually joining in with God's creations. When I remember a beautiful place and combine my memory with imagination, I am playing with God's creativity.

"Now when I look at the completed paintings, I return to these places with pleasure. And when other people enjoy the paintings, they bring their way of seeing and their imagination to what God has expressed through me."

Let the imagery of the following prayers be absorbed by your heart-mind.

Let yourself be called.

Invitation

You are being sent a secret message:
Everywhere it is revealed
Wake up!
Peer into the mirror,
Look through the window
Step outside
Dogs, cats, deer, birds, trees, flowers
God is calling, calling, calling.
Cast aside the outworn cloak of timidity
Immerse yourself in the waters
The flow of the ten thousand joys and sorrows.
Feel your skin caressed by the breeze
Let yourself be shaped by the Beloved.

Let a smile spread through your heartbeat

Laugh for no reason

Wonderful, wonderful, wonderful!

Singing and dancing await you.

We have time for nothing

But the truth.

❧

The Light is Beckoning

The Light is beckoning you
You yearn to expand into the warmth
The shadow whispers to you
Mystery and stillness await you
Wherever there is sunlight,
Also, there is shadow.

Stand under a tree
Say "Thank you, tree"
For shade and coolness
Press your ear to the tree
Listen, listen,
Tree wants to speak to you.

I heard my tree say,
"Your love gives me that special something
That makes my days happier."

So it is with Love.
Love everyone and everything
As much as you will.
Become Love itself
Until you become the Light,
Light and Shadow.

Light embracing shadow
Light revealing mystery
Like the shadow reflections
of moving water
On rocks by the river
Rippling with delight,
Shivering with ecstasy.

❧

Response-ability

How does God call to us? How do we know what our calling is in each phase of our life? How do we respond if we know there is more than one calling?

I have been learning to listen to God's voice through intuition – my body-sense of knowing. Intuitive knowledge, combined with intellect, is opening me to new perspectives. This brings forth a deep kind of pleasure.

We are given abilities by God to share with God, our world and ourselves. Responsibility is responding with ability.

A gift unfulfilled is like a present left wrapped.

Creative Calling

You are the thunder-roar of urging,
From within and beyond,
Calling me to stand on holy ground.

You have given me this time,
From the cry of the first inhale
To the sigh of the last exhale.
You define my time
With your essence.

May I listen to Your voice through intuition.
May I awaken to Your wisdom through learning.
May I delight in Your wonders with enthusiasm.
May I follow Your callings with passion.

Your presence forms my soul's yearning,
To create, shape and build,
To love, birth and nurture, to heal and repair,
To sing and dance, to serve and teach,
To be used well,
To reach out into this sacred universe,
And join you, Creator of Creation.

May I be the clay of Your formation,
The expression of Your imagination,
Your power, Your Divinity.

Guide my direction,

As my footsteps find their way.

May my thoughts and actions

Be in answer to Your callings.

🦎

III. STILLNESS AND MOVEMENT

Dance as Prayer

Dance is a body/mind/spirit connection that engages the soul in a way beyond words.

Improvised dance, with the consciousness of meditation, allows the logical mind to unhinge. Dance as prayer lets the ageless, infinite soul of the self move and breathe— into a kind of silence that pulses with the truth of the heart.

Ah, but some might say, "I am fearful of my dance — afraid to make a wrong step. I think my body is not graceful or beautiful enough." But do you think a jaguar leaps from a tree and then turns back to say, "That wasn't a very good leap. I should do it better"? No, because the jaguar leaps naturally.

So, too, it is human nature to dance. Remember when you were a child and your body was breathing and alive with the fun of each new movement — before you ever knew words like competition, graceful, or clumsy. That playful child is still in each of us, no matter our age, size, disposition, or condition. The place of dance and song, the instinct to dance, to move, is present in every stage of life, from infancy to elderhood. I have learned this from dancing with frail elders: The desire to move to music and to be playful in movement still exists even in those who have endured strokes and dementia.

There is no wrong way. Your dance is your prayer, your intimate connection with the Divine through the wondrous vehicle of your body.

Many think of dance as celebratory — as an expression of happiness. But true joy is wholeness. We have the opportunity to come into wholeness, to be healed by dance. Dance is the authentic movement that comes from the breath, the heart and the soul.

We can allow soul to move the muscles. This becomes the dance of one's truth in any given moment, because the fluidity of movement that offers limitless possibilities can come from the deepest place within. It can be small or large, soundless or vocal. It can be solo, with a partner or with a group.

Dance can be playful, silly, somber, exploratory, amazing. We can amaze ourselves with unexpected possibilities as we create movement in the moment.

But what if one is grief-stricken, if one's heart is broken open? Listen to what Rumi, the Sufi mystic poet, said:

Dancing is not rising to your feet painlessly
Like a whirl of dust blown about by the wind.
Dancing is when you rise above both worlds,
Tearing your heart to pieces and giving up your soul.

In the darkest times of my life, dance has been my deepest healing prayer. There is a sacred healing when I take my dance to the trees and the beach. Dancing on the earth and touching sky takes me beyond myself. Dancing in the water delights my dolphin-nature.

41

As I connect with myself, I feel a transporting of energy beyond self into the Divine, the moving, breathing, creative energy of the infinite universe.

I may come beseeching God from a hurting place, I may come burnt-out, confused, tormented. I may wish to dance exaltation and gratitude.

Dance as prayer does not have to be a big deal. It can be as simple as breathing in and out from your heart center and raising your arms in an open gesture. What happens when you raise your arms in this simple way? Can you feel that you up-lift your spirit? Can you feel a quality of presence, praise, and thanksgiving?

And when you move to the rhythm of your own inhale and exhale, can you feel how organically you connect with your self?

I do not know in what form God responds to prayer. I do know that by dancing our prayers, energy is transformed.

Take off your shoes and stand on holy ground.

Declare the holiness of this moment.

"A dance before the Blessed Holy One is prayer."

Baal Shem Tov

These meditations in stillness and movement have been created to help you integrate body, mind and spirit. Let yourself drop into the "I" voice of the speaker.

You can use them sitting in your chair, lying down or standing up. They can be done with music or simply to the rhythm of your own breath.

You may use them solo as daily meditation to awaken you. Or you may enjoy these body-prayers with another or with a group.

Let your dance lead you into deeper knowing.

Awakening: Meditation in Stillness

Breathing in
Opening to this day
Releasing to this moment in time
Creating the space for
Breathing in
And now,
Releasing the breath.

Letting my breath become easy
The simple focus of awareness.

Allowing breath to breathe me
Letting God's breath breathe me
Declaring that this is sacred space
This is holy ground
This place — in this time — here — now
Meeting the breath
The breath meeting me
Easily, effortlessly — with kindness

Infusing my breath with lovingkindness,
Breathing into my heart,
Into the center of the chest,
As if my heart is a sun
Radiating healing warmth all through me.

Breathing in the warmth of Love.
Allowing grace to caress me inwardly.
I exhale fully— allowing this sun to radiate
From my heart,
All through chest and back and shoulders,

Into my neck, noticing the connection of neck to jaw
Breathing into the space between the upper and lower teeth
Releasing into the dark space behind my eyes
Loosening the forehead and the back of the head.

•

Breathing in lovingkindness
Opening the mouth
Breathing out — an "ah" sound
Ah, sighing, giving my sigh to God.

And now again breathing into my heart
Creating more space in the back of my heart
The place between the shoulder blades
Allowing an unburdening of the shoulders
Sending warmth down my arms

Infusing compassion in all my joints
Elbows, wrists, fingers
Into the spaces between the fingers
And even beyond the fingers.

Bringing awareness back into my heart
Pulsing into the network of arteries and veins
All through cells and organs.

Throughout my belly and my pelvis
Well-being and kindness streaming
Into all the joints of my legs, feet, and toes
Creating more space between the toes.

Listening inwardly to the calling of my body
Lingering at the edges of any tightness
Pausing wherever there is pain or holding
Pausing wherever healing is called for.

Listening to the places in the mind
Where there are
Any thoughts, which keep me separated
From my true nature
Listening to the thoughts that keep me separated
From that which is always whole.

Creating this time now
To be totally embraced by Divine Love
To allow God's smile
To circulate through me
Finding my way into at-one-ment.

❧

Awakening: A Movement Meditation

In my own time, I rise to my feet
Making the connection of feet to earth
Drawing support from the earth as a tree
Up through my feet and legs
As if I could breathe from my feet
Letting my feet draw energy from the earth
Breathing an inner massage from feet
To the crown of my head
And back down again
Reaching outward through my branches
Arms lifting into the air and light
Circulating the energy up and down.

Gently beginning to move my head in my own way
Rolling to the inner music of breath.

And now shifting the weight from side to side
Softening the knees
Rocking, swaying, beginning to play.

Exploring the undulation of my spine
The connection of pelvis to neck and head
Finding the serpent in the spine
On the rhythm of the breath.

Letting the movement become larger
Expanding that rocking and shifting
Taking my arms with me into the space
As I reach out into the space
Letting my dance become prayer.

Reaching outward into the space around me
Arms lifting from the heart — on the breath —
And drawing the space in.
Reaching out for all that is Divine
Beyond
And within
Gathering in blessing.

Finding the wave of energy on the breath

That undulates through me

That wave-like energy where one movement

Moves into another

And another

Opening to the play of vibration
Allowing the Divine to dance through me.

Letting the Divine lead me
As the wave of energy plays upon the spine
•
I let God dance me.
Exploring circles around myself and around others
Little circles and bigger circles
Circling together
Circling the space of the room.

Dancing broken-ness and sorrow
Dancing wholeness and joy
Dancing with the Divine
The Divine dances me
Yes — Yes — Yes.

And now letting it become quieter
Awakening to the music of my heartbeat
My aliveness
The quickening of breath
Now beginning to slow.
Letting forth an "Ah" sound
"Ah"
From the center of my heart
"Ah"

•

Bringing the energy of the dance
Into the stillness of this moment
Drawing the energy
Into the space of my prayer.

May the power of this dance
This outpouring of Love
Bring healing to wherever
It is called for.

‹❧

Spaciousness

"Nothing begets wholeness in life better than a heartfelt sigh."   — Reb Nachman of Breslav

Breath is where we begin. For God is as close as the next breath. Ah, the breath....

God, lead me into the stillness
That I may find my inner dance.
I deepen into the breath
Meeting the longing of my heart.

Breathing in and breathing out, we are in a continual inner dance. The breath is the mediator of body, mind and spirit.. The word "*Ruach*" in Hebrew means breath, spirit and wind. Breath is the life-force of Spirit moving through us.

So start out by giving your sigh to God. To do that you have to let go of a big breath. Taking a big breath is not the key to relaxation, not if you hold it in or let it out in little anxious exhales. It is the letting go of the big breath, giving your sigh to God that leads to relaxation. In this sigh we empty ourselves of unnecessary holding, allowing for softening spaciousness.

We are perhaps crying, maybe even complaining to God in that sigh. We are letting go, emptying so that new fresh energy can enter our bodies. In this way we renew with Spirit. We renew our spirits.

Explore the breath of a spacious heart.
Open the space
Let the Light shine out.

54

Meditation on Spaciousness

Sighing, exhaling   Ah!

Let there be breath

Let there be breath around my heart

So that there also will be Light

Opening the space for myself

For whatever I am thinking, feeling, sensing

Without judgment

Releasing the holding and contraction

That forms the wall against the Light

And in the next exhale

I open the space for Divine Energy.

Moving gently into the unknown
Being with this time
In whatever form it takes in this moment . . .
. . . And in this moment . . .

•

Allowing more space in the darkness behind my eyes
More space in the upper and lower jaw
And into my neck and shoulders
Releasing unnecessary burden, unnecessary holding.
Opening the energy around my heart
So there is breath around my heart

Being aware of heart energy in the center of my chest
And the center of my back between the shoulder blades
Letting that space widen a little more
And letting that widening expand all through my back.

Opening the pelvis — breathing into my belly, my hips
Allowing the flow of energy to move
Through cells and organs.

Giving myself a little more spaciousness . . .

. . . Even a lot more spaciousness

Internally and outward too

Into the arms and hands, . . . the space between the fingers

Into the legs and feet, . . . the space between the toes.

Now, breathing into my neck and head

Turning in place — Lifting my arms.

Lifting my head.

Lifting my heart.

Let there be breath

So there will be Light

Ah…

꿍

IV. *SEARCHING ON THE PATH*

River of Compassion

The rushing waters of the river of compassion

Carve through the canyon of my soul

You answer prayers that are mute to my own ears

You bless me by holding me in your heart

You bless me by piercing my heart with Your Light.

Your Oneness merges me with all beings

You are with me always.

❧

Remembering to Pray

We remember God. We are in bliss. We swear we will always remember. Then, the phone rings or we're late for work or an old emotional wound is triggered.

We forget. We lose our way. We fall off the path to enlightenment. We forget that we do know how to pray.

We yearn to come home.

Dear God,

Distill me to pure essence

That I may hear your prayers for me.

Asking to Pray

Dear God,

Some days I do not know how to pray.

There are times when my inner noise is so turbulent

That I cannot even find my prayers.

Dear God,

There are days when I forget you,

When I forget who I truly am.

There are times when the marketplace is my universe.

There are times when scared energy fuels my little self,

And I forget the sacred energy of faith in you, my Source,

My vision narrows and I can barely see,

My ears are so full of chatter that I can hardly hear.

No wonder then that I forget

That I know how to pray.

Dear God,

Distill me to pure essence

That I may hear Your prayers for me.

Dear God,
Guide me into the silence
Where You await me.
Lead me in the music
Where You dance my body.
I am graced by Your breath in my ear
In the anguish of broken-ness,
And in the seeking of repair.
I am graced by Your breath in my ear
In the beauty you walk me through,
And in the ecstasy of aliveness.

Dear God,
Distill me to pure essence
That I may hear Your prayers for me.

Balance

With all the emotional storms of the human struggle, sometimes I need to just be at the still point of center.

Can I live with passionate commitment and also be in balance?

Whatever is happening right now, all that I name as good or bad, wondrous or terrible –

I pray for my heart to open to Love,

However it appears.

Prayer for Fearless Equanimity

Today, my God,

I pray to be spacious to the unfolding of Mystery,

That I may greet each moment

With courage and balance.

I cry out knowing that I do not know.

The only secret is Love

Which I am returned to again and again in many forms.

I pray for my heart to open to Love,

However it appears,

In the gatherings, the falling apart,

The swelling and the fading,

The birthing and the dying,

This moment and the passing of this moment

The pulse of All.

❧

Divine Mother

Sometimes I am awakened by the raucous call of the raven. The raven call may be in the form of a confrontation in an intimate relationship, an illness or perhaps a catastrophic situation. Or sometimes my awakening is more like the song sparrow before dawn, the words of a compassionate teacher or perhaps, the sweet music of poetry.

God is a Divine Mother enchanting me with love,
Cajoling me with laughter,
Gently and powerfully calling me home.

Silence all that deafens my heart

Silence all that deafens my heart
From hearing You
The noise has hastened me away from You
My passions struggle in a barren wilderness
Yet I am locked into this belly
This chamber of tears.

Now, in this holy now,
Hear my longing
I reach for You
In the night-time of separation

I ran and hid
And felt forsaken by You.
How is it that You always find me?
You who know my thoughts
Before I think

Even when I shiver from loneliness
Even when I have fragmented to pieces
You have not forgotten me.
Like a raven your call is insistent
Like a song sparrow your voice is sweet.

I have been testing You
Doubting your appearance
In the desert, in the city.
The visitor in the next room
Surely he could not be You.

Your laughter envelops me
In an instant
Your Divine Playfulness
Enchants me
I want to come home.

Root out all that separates me
From You
I want to live only
To remember You
Remember You.

❧

Courage and Faith

So much of what prevents joy in our lives is fear. We suffer from fear of creativity, fear of stepping beyond our limitations, fear of not being acceptable, fear of being lonely, as well as other fears that are unique to each of us.

It takes courage to observe the origins of fear, the layers of all that has frightened us and ultimately, to move through fear. Attention to this consciousness can lead to liberation from self-imposed suffering.

When layers of old, no longer useful emotion dissolve, there is, perhaps, a deep quiet where you may hear the "still, small voice within."

Your true essence that is Love desires you to live in the wholeness of your being. I believe there is a natural alignment – a harmony of body/mind and spirit that we innately know how to embrace and ultimately to become.

When we are challenged by a risk, sometimes we find courage from within ourselves in new, untried ways. We are given the opportunity to have faith in Energy greater than fear – as we step into the unknown.

Security is an illusion I attach myself to.
The next moment is always unknown.
Do I have the courage to live in joy?
Do I have the courage to laugh at myself?

En-Couragement

God,
Grant me the courage to see Your face
To see Your every face
To see my own face
And let my maskless face be seen.

Free me from the bondage of addiction
That I gain courage to be free.
Reveal to me courage of creativity
That I enter into new realms.

Guide my courage to be with my fear
To move through fear
Strengthening me in untried ways
That I become explorer, lover, artist.

Yield from my soul courage to imagine, to wonder
To dance, to sing, to revel in colors
To be sensual, in prayer and ecstasy
Even when it doesn't make sense.

Remove from me
All that hinders me from wholeness
So I become the truth of my being.

You grace me with the power
Of time and energy.
I receive You with an open heart.

ఈ

Faith into the Dark Spaces

The door is half-open,

Revealing darkness.

I cannot see what is beyond.

My Friend, infuse me with the courage

Of a spacious heart,

To step into the shadow.

Trembling, I ask for faith

For I do not know

What awaits me.

It all looks like blackness now.

Guide me with Your wisdom.

I am here.

V.PEACE AND HEALING

Let Peace Begin with Me

Peace is the foundation of the universe.

Peace is the alignment of the body. Peace is mindful calm. It is harmony in relationships and joy in solitude. Peace is the ecological inter-relationship of all beings to the planet. Peaceful alignment is the dynamic gravity that rotates the planets in the cosmos.

Let peace begin with me. By practicing loving-kindness toward myself, as if I am my own dear child, I am cultivating the roots of compassion.

This kindness will naturally bring me into inner harmony, extending outward to others. This process of self-healing will open me to empathy and forgiveness.

Praying for peace and affirming peace by action creates healing between you and others. Even when you are in despair that a relationship will "never" heal, experiment with these prayers.

Prayers for peace will change energy.

A Meditation:
Healing the Broken-ness

Giving my sigh to God....
Releasing the breath,
Releasing the holding
Of the ribs around the breath.

Like loosening a net around my heart,
Softening – gently – kindly
Giving my sigh to God.

And, now, being with myself in the stillness.
Deepening into the quiet movement of breath,
Allowing my breath to draw awareness
Deeper into my body,
Becoming aware of places of holding,
Of the places where pain has congealed.

Perhaps there has been shock
Where the breath is caught and doesn't quite let go.

Perhaps the wound is old or renewed
And there is a frozen place in my heart.

Wherever the energy is trapped,
For now, I just notice.

Listening to the sensation of energy,
Where energy moves freely and
Where there are obstacles.

For now - nothing to do - only breathing
Observing,   listening,   feeling…

The pulse of the stillness
So many times going to this wall of pain and retreating.
Now, I gently approach,
As much as I'm willing and able,
At this time,
To move through.

One step at a time
One breath at a time.

•

Breathing into the broken-ness,
Being with myself,
Being with all
That cries out for repair.

Allowing the breath
The in and out of breath
To bring me into wholeness
To be touched with holiness.

Prayer for Peace Within

In this moment
I call a truce within myself
And create the space for peace.

I allow my ribs expansion,
Letting go of the out-breath in surrender.
I lengthen my spine allowing strength and courage
Full expression.
My feet breathe support from the earth.

Breathing in and out
I create the space for peace with all beings,
Beginning with myself.
I allow Your stream of energy to flow freely through my body
That I may open to serenity.

Beloved Friend,
I ask to be restored to wholeness,
Healing all the fractures
That have led me away from You.

I ask to be re-joined in the Way of Love

That the hearts of all beings

Whom I have been divided from

Also may be brought into harmony.

I enter into joyful reunion with You,

Compassionate Creator of Peace.

❧

Prayer for Peace

There is a place
Between us
Where we will join
Where we will be made whole
Where we will be made One.

In the breath of the wind
And the ground of the earth
There is a place
Where our hearts will meet
Where we will touch
The Love that we are.

Sacred One
Teach us compassion
That we may heal one another.

❧

Transmission of Energy

Whether as a healer for others or as one who wants healing, I open to the infusion of holy energy. I become an open channel, attuning myself to the woundedness, the pain, the depression – whatever is out of alignment. I visualize the place of wholeness. I allow my hands, heart and mind to receive the transmission of healing energy that is all around, all through, all beyond.

Some may call this love. Some may call this God.

Healing

(For Self-healing)
Receiving your prayers
Receiving your blessings
With each breath I am drawing in your Goodness
Your love touches my pain
Your love heals and I am made whole
Your infinite love is streaming through my entire being.

(For Healing Another)
I am a channel for Your healing.
I reach out my hands
The energy of Your compassion fills my heart
Flowing through my hands
Touching the pain of this being

•

You and I, we are one
We are part of the All.
You and I, we are one.

Sabbath
Peace and Quiet

How wonderful to pause into the stillness. We let go of being a human doing and become a human being.

The most sacred of all holidays, Shabbat comes once a week.

We let go of work – of achievement – and all that is not achieved. We allow ourselves the un-conditional reward of just being who we truly are.

As we rest, we allow the muddy waters of continual activity to become still until the water of our body/mind becomes clear and calm. We wish each other Sabbath peace, "Shabbat Shalom."

My grandson Zachary joins me for Shabbat.

We gaze into the light of the darkness.

We let out a big letting-go sigh and breathe,

"Ah – peace and quiet."

Shabbat

As we greet You
We repose in Your Divine love

We merge into the blessing of Shabbat,
We rest in beauty.
We pause into the stillness
To celebrate our gratitude.
Peace and quiet
Peace and quiet.

In this sacred time we kindle lights,
Gazing into the light of the darkness.
Now is the time of drinking wine,
Celebrating the fullness of our cups of joy and sorrow.
We bless bread,
Remembering our nourishment and our hunger.
Feeding one another
We know how delicious
Is the sharing of our love and joy.
Peace and quiet
Peace and quiet.

God, You are our Source and our Home
We are filled with Your Love
For we are Your sweet children
Father... Mother... God... Beloved Friend.

We are held in Your arms in
Peace and quiet
Peace and quiet.

Shabbat Shalom.

Pure Water

Our blue planet circles in the galaxy. Our land is surrounded by water; our bodies are composed largely of water.

Surround me with water
And let it be pure.
Bathe my heart with daily healing
With water that itself does not need healing.

We are deeply, intrinsically connected with the elements.

We are the guardians of our
Earth, air, and waters.
Earth, air and waters - they are guardians of us.

Prayer for Healing Waters

O, God
Surround me with water
And let it be pure

Let me feel the drizzle of liquid on my arms
And the blessing of waterfall on my head

Surround me with water
And let it be pure

Shower me with cool wetness — salty or clear
Let water wash and cleanse
What needs to be forgotten

Surround me with water
And let it be pure

Bathe my heart with daily healing
With water that itself does not need healing

Bless the rain that joins the streams
Bless the streams that feed the rivers
Bless the rivers that pour into the seas

O, God

Surround me with water

And let it be pure.

‿ϖ

VI. *GRACE*

Grace

One day, in despair, I knelt in a garden. Moving into the yoga posture called Child's Position, I bent to the earth for support. I wept for all the loss I felt. At that moment, my back was brushed with gentle warmth, a sensation of invisible healing touch. In some deep way, I realized that I am not alone. I am graced.

A psychotherapy client who has been working very hard to let go of her addictions tells me that she has been freed. The destructive compulsions have left her. She feels that God has graced her.

Others have shared with me healing dreams in which tensions and fears in their lives have been resolved. These dreams were gifts from the unconscious, creating serenity in their attitudes and actions.

How does grace appear for you?

Grace from Unknown Places

Falling into grace
Surrendering to the matrix of Your heart
Bending closer to earthwomb
Smelling the scent of Your prayers in soil
Compost of yesterday's fragile leaves,
Tangled roots,
Seeds of secret promises
Your longing,
Your prayers for the miraculous
Order of things.

Fingers reaching out to mountain garlands
You touch eyes with celebrations of purple
Flags of lupine and larkspur.

Tree waits here, old and strong,
Tree absorbing the dissolution of anguish,
Receiving hunger for you, my Beloved Friend,
Into the holding of its trunk.
I whisper. I wait. I listen for You,
You who speak in a thousand tongues.

You answer.
You, God, are laughing
Answering with a magical joke
You sometimes pray with gentle laughter!
You, tree, you laugh with me.
Leaves are loving me,
Branches are blessing me,
Sunshine is lavishing laughter on grasses,
The grasses that perfume the air
With Your prayers of ecstasy.

Oh, God

Your love remedies all that is fragile and forlorn

You lift me

You hold me

You turn me around

You heal me.

I am yours.

Silence

Let me be with You in silence
Releasing into the surround of Your gentle grace.
My prayer needs no tongue to speak
For the yearnings of my mute heart
Are already heard by You.

In timeless quiet.
As a feather landing on yellowed grass,
As the dust onhte butterfly wing,
As the speck of pollen on the leg of the bee. Your voice is heard.

I am finding my own way to speak with You,
Sometimes, it is just my footfalls on the earth.
Hear my prayers.

౭ॐ

Breath and Being

One summer day, while feeling the cool grass on my bare feet, I wanted to create simple prayers, devoid of big words and large concepts. What follows are prayers of simplicity.

Here I Am

I am here.

I breathe your breath…

Standing on this earth

Reaching upward I touch sky…

Here I am God

Here in this moment….

I ask for sacred emptiness

Only this breath, this Time, this Space

Being here with You.

❧

Thirst

I thirst for the sweet water of Your love

I hunger for the taste of Your sustenance

Clothe me in the grace of Your forgiveness

May I be worthy of this journey.

❧

Beloved Friend

I am a child comforted by You,
Loving Mother, Knowing Father,
Beloved Friend,
I rest in the safety of your embrace
Your Love provides me with all I need.
You are all I am.

VII. *IN MEMORIAM*

Emptiness and Fullness

The following meditations are on connection with those who have passed over.

The first is a meditation on emptiness and fullness. Two of the ways our hearts are opened are when we fall in love and the other is when we grieve for the loss of one we love.

Can we feel the fullness of love and the emptiness of loss at the same time?

First, I encourage you to breathe gently, to connect consciously with your breath and your body. Instead of contracting against the pain of sorrow, breathe into the pain. Instead of contracting the muscles in an attempt to push away the feelings, try softening into the broken heart. Let yourself be cleansed by tears, rather than damming up their energy.

And dance. Move the energy. As you do, images may come and new responses may be engaged.

There is no use pretending that we have control over grief. Grief seems to have a mind of its own, showing up unannounced, having its way with us.

Better to dance with our sorrow, breathe into brokenness, strengthening our gladness with our grief.

In Memoriam:
A Guided Meditation
on
Grief and Loss

Breathing in and out
Breathing into the center of my heart
My spiritual heart in the center of my chest
Into the space between the shoulder blades in my back.

Exhaling with a sigh
Giving my sigh to God
Ah . . . . yes
Letting go of the tightness around my heart
And behind my eyes.

Allowing God's healing to warm
Back, head, neck, shoulders
To surround me in Its embrace.

Breathing in healing energy, warmth and light
Like a gentle candle illuminating the dark corners of a cave
I bring God into the sorrow, the loss,
And where there is fear and anger,
I surround my tight heart with God's love.

As much as I'm able and willing at this time
Allowing Love to warm my heart
As I breathe out
I'm sending this healing light
Throughout my belly and back
To the space between the ribs
To the tears and wounds of loss.

If doubt and resistance arise,
If fear of the pain arises
I surround *these* feelings with healing light
Being just where I am.

Dropping down into the recesses of my heart
Sitting and being with my own heart
Hearing the calling of my own heart —
Be with me. Don't leave me. Be with me.

Can I let go of designing my grief,
Imagining I have control?
Perhaps I can dance with my sorrow,
Allowing the pain of grieving to move through my body
Strengthening my gladness with my grief.

Is it possible to feel my heart both empty and full
At the same time?
I yearn, in sorrow,
For the loss of you.

I feel incompleteness in what I still wish
To say, share, and do together.
I ache
With the unfinished sentences
Still on my tongue.

I am filled with the blessing of love shared
Everyone who has ever loved me
Everyone I have ever loved
You have presence within me.
I celebrate the sweetness
Of what we have known of life together.

•

Empty and full heart –
This is healing time now.
A time to join in spirit with you
To let my heart speak
Into the spaces between the words.
To listen, in the silence,
To the message you have for me.

•

Opening my heart a little wider.
To where there is suffering elsewhere in the world
Sending this healing light outward.
Compassion, love, peace,
Just maybe my healing will
become a beacon of light.

Here I am, God.

In this emptiness,

In this fullness.

Your sacred presence blesses me.

I meet You now.

Be with me.

ॐ

In Her Stead

In the Jewish tradition, Kaddish is the mourner's prayer. In sacred words in the language of Aramaic, the chanting begins:

"*Yit-gadel ve-yit-kadash shmei raba.*"

"We enhance and sanctify Your presence
In the world of Your creation."

The prayer never mentions death or even alludes to the departed one; it is completely a prayer of adoration of the Holy One, a celebration of the continual shower of blessing and of God's wisdom and goodness beyond human understanding.

Though we commonly think of saying Kaddish in honor of those who have passed over into the realm of death, we are actually saying Kaddish in the stead of the departed one who can no longer speak these words.

One day I walked into a garden and thought how my mother would have loved these dahlias. And, so, I smell and partake of delight in them now in her stead, remembering her delight in life. How she said Kaddish with the joy in living she expressed. How she adored God with her smiles, her paintings and her love for us – my father, my brother and me.

Kaddish for My Mother

Gone into the realm of death,

You cast your essence through me

Light as mist

Deep as tree-roots.

I say Kaddish for you

Because your are not here

Not here

To praise God for impossible possibilities.

You left your thick, impasto canvases

Still wet with magentas and cerulean.

Now I pick up the brush

And say Kaddish

For you who can no longer paint.

I swim lakes and say
The Kaddish of delight
In the marvel of movement
In praise of aliveness of body
For you are not here
To be blessed by water.
There you are, In that 3"x 3" black and white photo,
A big smile saying Kaddish to me
Still blessing me.
Still blessing me.

I walk through a garden of
Dahlias, columbines, honeysuckles,
Saying Kaddish in your stead
You would have wanted to paint these flowers
The flowers who say Kaddish for you
Blessing of color and fragrance.

Perhaps, though you cannot mouth
The words of praise,
Your soul has been saying Kaddish all along
Praising God, showering blessing on me
On my children and my children's children.

For together we are saying,
"God,
We celebrate, rejoice, acclaim and adore
Your sacred presence
Beyond all poetry and song
Name beyond names,
We bless you as you bless us.
And let us say:
It is."

For Angie

Two days after my "surrogate" mother, Angie, died, she spoke these words to and through me. I experienced the aliveness of her soul.

Now when I miss her, I know she is knocking on the door of my heart, and my tears of mourning turn to joy as I realize again the blessing she was and still is in my life.

Good-bye, I'm here

So tired, so weary

So hard to breathe

The weight upon my chest.

Let me rest,

Let me go ....

Letting go, letting go.......

Going over, between the blue doors

Into no-where,

Into every-where.

Giddy with joy-

Laughing and crying.

Laughter comes easily.

This is fun.

Spinning, floating….

I am a child on a swing,

A feather in the wind,

A cloud in the sky….

Light — I am Light

And here is God.

Hello, God,

I've been wanting to see you.

I've been with you all along.

I know that.

Now, I am in the place of no place,

I am gone.

Good-bye everyone.

I am here. Good-bye.

I am here

Good-bye…I am here.

I am gone.

I am here.

I love you

Yet,

No more "I."

No more "you."

Only Love,

Dissolved into Love,

Becoming Love,

Being Love,

Love so pure.

No more "I." No more "you."

Only Love,

The radiant essence that I was moving towards

My whole life.

The place of no place.

Only Love that is Everywhere.

Only Love.

❧

Connection

How inter-woven we all are – with our past, with our future, with one another, with all beings. We form one another in ways beyond imagining, often beneath the level of consciousness.

We are each a thread in the greater fabric of the All.

The Weaving

You have never really left me
I thought I was alone - so lonely
No more you
To touch, to feel
Your voice had left my ear.
But, no, not really
I can hear you
I do hear you
You still hold me
And I hold you.
I hear now with different ears
See with different eyes
Ah yes, my heart has widened now
Including all of you
All of us
For it is not my heart at all
But God's heart.

We are always loving one another

You and me, ancestors, grandparents

Mother, father, children

Lovers, friends, pets.

We are so close

As real as my breath

As real as my heartbeat.

More than I ever could have imagined

We are one.

I am a thread

In the weaving of the prayer-shawl of life

We form one another.

And the fringes?

Oh yes, those are the ones

Yet to come.

VIII. PRAISE & THANKSGIVING

Gratitude

It was Thanksgiving. And it was one of the first days I taught in a nursing home – charged with the mission of mental and physical stimulation for frail elders. I asked these weak, wheelchair-bound, half-paralyzed people slowly losing their memory, "What are you thankful for?" Even as I asked this question, the skeptic in me was thinking, "What could these poor, old people be grateful for?"

But, as if waking from a sleep, the answers came back with vigor:

"Health!"
"My children!"
"My parents!"
"The variety of my life!"
"The people who change our diapers!"
"Being here!"

What an incredible teaching I received from these wise ones.

As we finished writing a group prayer on Gratitude, I could feel a palpable shift of energy in the room. So I asked, "What is it about being grateful that makes us feel so good?"

And Verna answered, a lilt in her voice, "It's like coming home."

Gratitude is the fountain of healing. Gratitude changes perception and opens up creative possibility. What are you grateful for in this moment?

Dance of Thanksgiving

The whole world sings Your praise
Alive with the dance of Thanksgiving
Our hearts overflow with Your shower of blessings
It is good,
It is good.

Changing winds breathe Your breath
You turn the earth toward the light of day
And reveal the stars of night
It is good,
It is good.

You shape Yourself into myriad forms
Motion of molecules, waves of water
Dance to the pace of Your rhythm
It is good,
It is good.

Whales and fish swim to Your harmony

Trees and mountains ascend to Your glory

Deer leap through forest

It is good,

It is good.

Crystal of snowflake, roaming of buffalo, eyes of mother
and child, smile of dolphin, fragrance of narcissus,
tail of peacock, ripening of pomegranate.

Abundant, gracious earth
We sing and dance Your praise
Thank you, Thank you – In joy we sound out
It is good,
It is good.

You create us as caregivers of one another
Guardians of the family of creation
The interweave of Your divine design
It is good,
It is good.

May we sow and reap
Gather and re-generate
Full of care, thankfulness and wisdom
It is good,
It is good.

Blessed God,
Name Beyond Names

I am summoned to You in this place, this time
For You are my God

You inhabit my body with a pure soul
You open my mouth in praise of You

You wrench me free from the shackles of old sorrows
You awaken me and transmute my pain into the gift of sages

You call to me in sweetest song to walk Your walk
And dance Your dance

You beckon me into rivers and seas
Where I swim in the pleasure of Your waters

You weave me into the fabric of all living creations
All the ancestors and all those who will come

You heal me in Your mercy
Blessing my head with grace

You are the beating of the heart
And the withdrawal of breath

You are the seed's knowing of its blossom
And the fruit's containing of the seed

You are the laws of the light and the darkness
You are the axis of the turning of the Earth

You lift me from the dust into the stars
Together we are spread throughout the Infinite

I offer my whole self in gratitude
For all that my eyes and ears delight in
And for all that I may not yet see, hear nor understand

I praise You for all the love, healing and compassion
That we receive
And for all the Love and blessing
Which we have yet to receive

I pause into this moment to bring to heart
Each blessing of life

I uplift my heart in gladness for Your magnificence
Which is
Continuous, extended
Everywhere
Beyond all time

You are our God

Our Source

Our One.

❧

Dancing with the Divine
February, 2002

I had long led guided meditations, gentle imagery that engage people in the process of body and breath awareness as the meditations in the chapter called "Stillness and Movement" Then, one day while discussing a concept of a book of guided imagery with Rabbi Stan, I heard these words come out of my mouth: "You know, I think there's a book of *prayers* here, too!"

These words struck me as awesome. To write original prayers speaking directly to God seemed a daunting task. Could I be that bold? Stan responded with a knowing smile, "Of course."

I prayed now that as I had been given the vision to see the path, I'd also be given the courage to walk upon it. The act of producing the book became an embodiment of the prayers themselves, a place for me to wrestle with fear and faith.

The pendulum of my mind swung from "Who do you think you are to write a book of prayers?" to "God is calling, calling, calling."

When I answered to this resounding directive, I found myself resting in what felt like deep truth. I know I was being asked to write this book..

Some days I would walk around the house for an hour looking for just the thought - the word that would say it just right; other times there would be a flow like water. I was being "inspirited," in a new way. The process became very intuitive – just the simple act of deep listening and the solitude of pen and paper.

Addendum

It is now almost ten years since the first printing of Dancing with the Divine. After writing this book from my intuitive heart, I thought I needed the research and the discipline of investigating my Jewish heritage. I have studied Hebrew and taken a prayer leadership training - the Davennen Leadership Training Institute through Aleph –Alliance for Jewish Renewal. I have led Shabbat services as well as holidays for Older Adults.

In addition, there is a second book –*And You Shall Be A Blessing.* And, perhaps a third one- my responses to liturgy, is simmering on the fire of creation.

My interest in the poetry of prayer continues. I am still opposed to rote prayer that is said for the sake of righteousness. I would rather have one word said in truth than a whole book of liturgy recited without heart. And so I will boldly attempt more play with words from my truth, as best I can.

Dance as prayer continues to be my faithful companion. My body is riding gracefully over the waves of time and space. For this I am humbly grateful.

Santa Monica California   February 6, 2011

I am finding my own way to speak with You,
Sometimes, it is just my footfalls on the earth.
Hear my prayers.

☙